KU-168-332

WAR IS
A RACKET

By General Smedley D. Butler

Reprint Edition by Dauphin Publications, 2018

ISBN: 9781939438584

dauphin publications

General Butler

- Born: West Chester, Pa., July 30, 1881
- Educated: Haverford School
- Married: Ethel C. Peters, of Philadelphia, June 30, 1905
- Awarded two congressional medals of honor:
    1. Capture of Vera Cruz, Mexico, 1914
    2. Capture of Ft. Riviere, Haiti, 1917
- Distinguished service medal, 1919
- Major General - United States Marine Corps
- Retired Oct. 1, 1931
- On leave of absence to act as director of Dept. of Safety, Philadelphia, 1932
- Lecturer — 1930's
- Republican Candidate for Senate, 1932
- Died at Naval Hospital, Philadelphia, June 21, 1940

For more information about Major General Butler, contact the United States Marine Corps.

Table of Contents

Title   Page

CHAPTER ONE

War Is A Racket

WAR is a racket. It always has been.

It is possibly the oldest, easily the most profitable, surely the most vicious. It is the only one international in scope. It is the only one in which the profits are reckoned in dollars and the losses in lives.

A racket is best described, I believe, as something that is not what it seems to the majority of the people. Only a small "inside" group knows what it is about. It is conducted for the benefit of the very few, at the expense of the very many. Out of war a few people make huge fortunes.

In the World War [I] a mere handful garnered the profits of the conflict. At least 21,000 new millionaires and billionaires were made in the United States during the World War. That many admitted their huge blood gains in their income tax returns. How many other war millionaires falsified their tax returns no one knows.

How many of these war millionaires shouldered a rifle? How many of them dug a trench? How many of them knew what it meant to go hungry in a rat-infested dug-out? How many of them spent sleepless, frightened nights, ducking shells and shrapnel and machine gun bullets? How many of them parried a bayonet thrust of an enemy? How many of them were wounded or killed in battle?

Out of war nations acquire additional territory, if they are victorious. They just take it. This newly acquired territory promptly is exploited by the few — the selfsame few who wrung dollars out of blood in the war. The general public shoulders the bill.

And what is this bill?

This bill renders a horrible accounting. Newly placed gravestones. Mangled bodies. Shattered minds. Broken hearts and homes. Economic instability. Depression and all its attendant miseries. Back-breaking taxation for generations and generations.

For a great many years, as a soldier, I had a suspicion that war was a racket; not until I retired to civil life did I fully realize it. Now that I see the international war clouds gathering, as they are today, I must face it and speak out.

Again they are choosing sides. France and Russia met and agreed to stand side by side. Italy and Austria hurried to make a similar agreement. Poland and Germany cast sheep's eyes at each other, forgetting for the nonce [one unique occasion], their dispute over the Polish Corridor.

The assassination of King Alexander of Jugoslavia [Yugoslavia] complicated matters. Jugoslavia and Hungary, long bitter enemies, were almost at each other's throats. Italy was ready to jump in. But France was waiting. So was Czechoslovakia. All of them are looking ahead to war. Not the people — not those who fight and pay and die — only those who foment wars and remain safely at home to profit.

There are 40,000,000 men under arms in the world today, and our statesmen and diplomats have the temerity to say that war is not in the making.

Hell's bells! Are these 40,000,000 men being trained to be dancers?

Not in Italy, to be sure. Premier Mussolini knows what they are being trained for. He, at least, is frank enough to speak out. Only the other day, Il Duce in "International Conciliation," the publication of the Carnegie Endowment for International Peace, said:

"And above all, Fascism, the more it considers and observes the future and the development of humanity quite apart from political considerations of the moment, believes neither in the possibility nor the utility of perpetual peace. . . . War alone brings up to

its highest tension all human energy and puts the stamp of nobility upon the people who have the courage to meet it."

Undoubtedly Mussolini means exactly what he says. His well-trained army, his great fleet of planes, and even his navy are ready for war — anxious for it, apparently. His recent stand at the side of Hungary in the latter's dispute with Jugoslavia showed that. And the hurried mobilization of his troops on the Austrian border after the assassination of Dollfuss showed it too. There are others in Europe too whose sabre rattling presages war, sooner or later.

Herr Hitler, with his rearming Germany and his constant demands for more and more arms, is an equal if not greater menace to peace. France only recently increased the term of military service for its youth from a year to eighteen months.

Yes, all over, nations are camping in their arms. The mad dogs of Europe are on the loose. In the Orient the maneuvering is more adroit. Back in 1904, when Russia and Japan fought, we kicked out our old friends the Russians and backed Japan. Then our very generous international bankers were financing Japan. Now the trend is to poison us against the Japanese. What does the "open door" policy to China mean to us? Our trade with China is about $90,000,000 a year. Or the Philippine Islands? We have spent about

$600,000,000 in the Philippines in thirty-five years and we (our bankers and industrialists and speculators) have private investments there of less than $200,000,000.

Then, to save that China trade of about $90,000,000, or to protect these private investments of less than $200,000,000 in the Philippines, we would be all stirred up to hate Japan and go to war — a war that might well cost us tens of billions of dollars, hundreds of thousands of lives of Americans, and many more hundreds of thousands of physically maimed and mentally unbalanced men.

Of course, for this loss, there would be a compensating profit — fortunes would be made. Millions and billions of dollars would be piled up. By a few. Munitions makers. Bankers. Ship builders. Manufacturers. Meat packers. Speculators. They would fare well.

Yes, they are getting ready for another war. Why shouldn't they? It pays high dividends.

But what does it profit the men who are killed? What does it profit their mothers and sisters, their wives and their sweethearts? What does it profit their children?

What does it profit anyone except the very few to whom war means huge profits?

Yes, and what does it profit the nation?

Take our own case. Until 1898 we didn't own a bit of territory outside the mainland of North America. At that time our national debt was a little more than $1,000,000,000. Then we became "internationally minded." We forgot, or shunted aside, the advice of the Father of our country. We forgot George Washington's warning about "entangling alliances." We went to war. We acquired outside territory. At the end of the World War period, as a direct result of our fiddling in international affairs, our national debt had jumped to over $25,000,000,000. Our total favorable trade balance during the twenty-five-year period was about $24,000,000,000. Therefore, on a purely bookkeeping basis, we ran a little behind year for year, and that foreign trade might well have been ours without the wars.

It would have been far cheaper (not to say safer) for the average American who pays the bills to stay out of foreign entanglements. For a very few this racket, like bootlegging and other underworld rackets, brings fancy profits, but the cost of operations is always transferred to the people — who do not profit.

CHAPTER TWO

Who Makes The Profits?

The World War, rather our brief participation in it, has cost the United States some $52,000,000,000. Figure it out. That means $400 to every American man, woman, and child. And we haven't paid the debt yet. We are paying it, our children will pay it, and our children's children probably still will be paying the cost of that war.

The normal profits of a business concern in the United States are six, eight, ten, and sometimes twelve percent. But war-time profits — ah! that is another matter — twenty, sixty, one hundred, three hundred, and even eighteen hundred percent — the sky is the limit. All that traffic will bear. Uncle Sam has the money. Let's get it.

Of course, it isn't put that crudely in war time. It is dressed into speeches about patriotism, love of country, and "we must all put our shoulders to the wheel," but the profits jump and leap and skyrocket — and are safely pocketed. Let's just take a few examples:

Take our friends the du Ponts, the powder people — didn't one of them testify before a Senate committee recently that their powder won the war? Or saved the world for democracy? Or something? How did they do in the war? They were a patriotic corporation. Well, the average earnings of the du Ponts for the period 1910 to 1914 were $6,000,000 a year. It wasn't much, but the du Ponts managed to get along on it. Now let's look at their average yearly profit during the war years, 1914 to 1918. Fifty-eight million dollars a year profit we find! Nearly ten times that of normal times, and the profits of normal times were pretty good. An increase in profits of more than 950 percent.

Take one of our little steel companies that patriotically shunted aside the making of rails and girders and bridges to manufacture war materials. Well, their 1910-1914 yearly earnings averaged $6,000,000. Then came the war. And, like loyal citizens, Bethlehem Steel promptly turned to munitions making. Did their profits jump — or did they let Uncle Sam in for a bargain? Well, their 1914-1918 average was $49,000,000 a year!

Or, let's take United States Steel. The normal earnings during the five-year period prior to the war were $105,000,000 a year. Not bad. Then along came the war and up went the profits. The average yearly profit for the period 1914-1918 was $240,000,000. Not bad.

There you have some of the steel and powder earnings. Let's look at something else. A little copper, perhaps. That always does well in war times.

Anaconda, for instance. Average yearly earnings during the pre-war years 1910-1914 of $10,000,000. During the war years 1914-1918 profits leaped to $34,000,000 per year.

Or Utah Copper. Average of $5,000,000 per year during the 1910-1914 period. Jumped to an average of $21,000,000 yearly profits for the war period.

Let's group these five, with three smaller companies. The total yearly average profits of the pre-war period 1910-1914 were $137,480,000. Then along came the war. The average yearly profits for this group skyrocketed to $408,300,000.

A little increase in profits of approximately 200 percent.

Does war pay? It paid them. But they aren't the only ones. There are still others. Let's take leather.

9

For the three-year period before the war the total profits of Central Leather Company were $3,500,000. That was approximately $1,167,000 a year. Well, in 1916 Central Leather returned a profit of $15,000,000, a small increase of 1,100 percent. That's all. The General Chemical Company averaged a profit for the three years before the war of a little over $800,000 a year. Came the war, and the profits jumped to $12,000,000. a leap of 1,400 percent.

International Nickel Company — and you can't have a war without nickel — showed an increase in profits from a mere average of $4,000,000 a year to $73,000,000 yearly. Not bad? An increase of more than 1,700 percent.

American Sugar Refining Company averaged $2,000,000 a year for the three years before the war. In 1916 a profit of $6,000,000 was recorded.

Listen to Senate Document No. 259. The Sixty-Fifth Congress, reporting on corporate earnings and government revenues. Considering the profits of 122 meat packers, 153 cotton manufacturers, 299 garment makers, 49 steel plants, and 340 coal producers during the war. Profits under 25 percent were exceptional. For instance the coal companies made between 100 percent and 7,856 percent on their capital stock during the war. The Chicago packers doubled and tripled their earnings.

And let us not forget the bankers who financed the great war. If anyone had the cream of the profits it was the bankers. Being partnerships rather than incorporated organizations, they do not have to report to stockholders. And their profits were as secret as they were immense. How the bankers made their millions and their billions I do not know, because those little secrets never become public — even before a Senate investigatory body.

But here's how some of the other patriotic industrialists and speculators chiseled their way into war profits.

Take the shoe people. They like war. It brings business with abnormal profits. They made huge profits on sales abroad to our allies. Perhaps, like the munitions manufacturers and armament makers, they also sold to the enemy. For a dollar is a dollar whether it comes from Germany or from France. But they did well by Uncle Sam too. For instance, they sold Uncle Sam 35,000,000 pairs of hobnailed service shoes. There were 4,000,000 soldiers. Eight pairs, and more, to a soldier. My regiment during the war had only one pair to a soldier. Some of these shoes probably are still in existence. They were good shoes. But when the war was over Uncle Sam has a matter of 25,000,000 pairs left over. Bought — and paid for. Profits recorded and pocketed.

There was still a lot of leather left. So the leather people sold your Uncle Sam hundreds of thousands of McClellan saddles for the cavalry. But there wasn't any American cavalry overseas! Somebody had to get rid of this leather, however. Somebody had to make a profit in it — so we had a lot of McClellan saddles. And we probably have those yet.

Also somebody had a lot of mosquito netting. They sold your Uncle Sam 20,000,000 mosquito nets for the use of the soldiers overseas. I suppose the boys were expected to put it over them as they tried to sleep in muddy trenches — one hand scratching cooties on their backs and the other making passes at scurrying rats. Well, not one of these mosquito nets ever got to France!

Anyhow, these thoughtful manufacturers wanted to make sure that no soldier would be without his mosquito net, so 40,000,000 additional yards of mosquito netting were sold to Uncle Sam.

There were pretty good profits in mosquito netting in those days, even if there were no mosquitoes in France. I suppose, if the war had lasted just a little longer, the enterprising mosquito netting manufacturers would have sold your Uncle Sam a couple of consignments of mosquitoes to plant in France so that more mosquito netting would be in order.

Airplane and engine manufacturers felt they, too, should get their just profits out of this war. Why not? Everybody else was getting theirs. So $1,000,000,000 — count them if you live long enough — was spent by Uncle Sam in building airplane engines that never left the ground! Not one plane, or motor, out of the billion dollars worth ordered, ever got into a battle in France. Just the same the manufacturers made their little profit of 30, 100, or perhaps 300 percent.

Undershirts for soldiers cost 14¢ [cents] to make and uncle Sam paid 30¢ to 40¢ each for them — a nice little profit for the undershirt manufacturer. And the stocking manufacturer and the uniform manufacturers and the cap manufacturers and the steel helmet manufacturers — all got theirs.

Why, when the war was over some 4,000,000 sets of equipment — knapsacks and the things that go to fill them — crammed warehouses on this side. Now they are being scrapped because the regulations have changed the contents. But the manufacturers collected their wartime profits on them — and they will do it all over again the next time.

There were lots of brilliant ideas for profit making during the war.

One very versatile patriot sold Uncle Sam twelve dozen 48-inch wrenches. Oh, they were very nice wrenches. The only trouble was that there was only one nut ever made that was large enough for these wrenches. That is the one that holds the turbines at Niagara Falls. Well, after Uncle Sam had bought them and the manufacturer had pocketed the profit, the wrenches were put on freight cars and shunted all around the United States in an effort to find a use for them. When the Armistice was signed it was indeed a sad blow to the wrench manufacturer. He was just about to make some nuts to fit the wrenches. Then he planned to sell these, too, to your Uncle Sam.

Still another had the brilliant idea that colonels shouldn't ride in automobiles, nor should they even ride on horseback. One has probably seen a picture of Andy Jackson riding in a buckboard. Well, some 6,000 buckboards were sold to Uncle Sam for the use of colonels! Not one of them was used. But the buckboard manufacturer got his war profit.

The shipbuilders felt they should come in on some of it, too. They built a lot of ships that made a lot of profit. More than $3,000,000,000 worth. Some of the ships were all right. But $635,000,000 worth of them were made of wood and wouldn't float! The seams opened up — and they sank. We paid for them, though. And somebody pocketed the profits.

It has been estimated by statisticians and economists and researchers that the war cost your Uncle Sam $52,000,000,000. Of this sum, $39,000,000,000 was expended in the actual war itself. This expenditure yielded $16,000,000,000 in profits. That is how the 21,000 billionaires and millionaires got that way. This $16,000,000,000 profits is not to be sneezed at. It is quite a tidy sum. And it went to a very few.

The Senate (Nye) committee probe of the munitions industry and its wartime profits, despite its sensational disclosures, hardly has scratched the surface.

Even so, it has had some effect. The State Department has been studying "for some time" methods of keeping out of war. The War Department suddenly decides it has a wonderful plan to spring. The Administration names a committee —with the War and Navy Departments ably represented under the chairmanship of a Wall Street speculator — to limit profits in war time. To what extent isn't suggested. Hmmm. Possibly the profits of 300 and 600 and 1,600 percent of those who turned blood into gold in the World War would be limited to some smaller figure.

Apparently, however, the plan does not call for any limitation of losses — that is, the losses of those who fight the war. As far as I have been able to ascertain there is nothing in the scheme to limit a soldier to the loss of but one eye, or one arm, or to limit his wounds to one or two or three. Or to limit the loss of life.

There is nothing in this scheme, apparently, that says not more than 12 percent of a regiment shall be wounded in battle, or that not more than 7 percent in a division shall be killed.

Of course, the committee cannot be bothered with such trifling matters.

CHAPTER THREE

Who Pays The Bills?

Who provides the profits — these nice little profits of 20, 100, 300, 1,500 and 1,800 percent? We all pay them — in taxation. We paid the bankers their profits when we bought Liberty Bonds at $100.00 and sold them back at $84 or $86 to the bankers. These bankers collected $100 plus. It was a simple manipulation. The bankers control the security marts. It was easy for them to depress the price of these bonds. Then all of us — the people — got frightened and sold the bonds at $84 or $86. The bankers bought them. Then these same bankers stimulated a boom and government bonds went to par — and above. Then the bankers collected their profits.

But the soldier pays the biggest part of the bill.

If you don't believe this, visit the American cemeteries on the battlefields abroad. Or visit any of the veteran's hospitals in the United States. On a tour of the country, in the midst of which I am at the time of this writing, I have visited eighteen government hospitals for veterans. In them are a total of about 50,000 destroyed men — men who were the pick of

17

the nation eighteen years ago. The very able chief surgeon at the government hospital; at Milwaukee, where there are 3,800 of the living dead, told me that mortality among veterans is three times as great as among those who stayed at home.

Boys with a normal viewpoint were taken out of the fields and offices and factories and classrooms and put into the ranks. There they were remolded; they were made over; they were made to "about face"; to regard murder as the order of the day. They were put shoulder to shoulder and, through mass psychology, they were entirely changed. We used them for a couple of years and trained them to think nothing at all of killing or of being killed.

Then, suddenly, we discharged them and told them to make another "about face"! This time they had to do their own readjustment, sans [without] mass psychology, sans officers' aid and advice and sans nation-wide propaganda. We didn't need them anymore. So we scattered them about without any "three-minute" or "Liberty Loan" speeches or parades. Many, too many, of these fine young boys are eventually destroyed, mentally, because they could not make that final "about face" alone.

In the government hospital in Marion, Indiana, 1,800 of these boys are in pens! Five hundred of them in a barracks with steel bars and wires all around outside the buildings and on the porches. These already have been mentally destroyed. These boys don't even look like human beings. Oh, the looks on their faces! Physically, they are in good shape; mentally, they are gone.

There are thousands and thousands of these cases, and more and more are coming in all the time. The tremendous excitement of the war, the sudden cutting off of that excitement — the young boys couldn't stand it.

That's a part of the bill. So much for the dead — they have paid their part of the war profits. So much for the mentally and physically wounded — they are paying now their share of the war profits. But the others paid, too — they paid with heartbreaks when they tore themselves away from their firesides and their families to don the uniform of Uncle Sam — on which a profit had been made. They paid another part in the training camps where they were regimented and drilled while others took their jobs and their places in the lives of their communities. The paid for it in the trenches where they shot and were shot; where they were hungry for days at a time; where they slept in the mud and the cold and in the rain — with the moans and shrieks of the dying for a horrible lullaby.

But don't forget — the soldier paid part of the dollars and cents bill too.

Up to and including the Spanish-American War, we had a prize system, and soldiers and sailors fought for money. During the Civil War they were paid bonuses, in many instances, before they went into service. The government, or states, paid as high as $1,200 for an enlistment. In the Spanish-American War they gave prize money. When we captured any vessels, the soldiers all got their share — at least, they were supposed to. Then it was found that we could reduce the cost of wars by taking all the prize money and keeping it, but conscripting [drafting] the soldier anyway. Then soldiers couldn't bargain for their labor, Everyone else could bargain, but the soldier couldn't.

Napoleon once said,

"All men are enamored of decorations . . . they positively hunger for them."

So by developing the Napoleonic system — the medal business — the government learned it could get soldiers for less money, because the boys liked to be decorated. Until the Civil War there were no medals. Then the Congressional Medal of Honor was handed out. It made enlistments easier. After the Civil War no new medals were issued until the Spanish-American War.

In the World War, we used propaganda to make the boys accept conscription. They were made to feel ashamed if they didn't join the army.

So vicious was this war propaganda that even God was brought into it. With few exceptions our clergymen joined in the clamor to kill, kill, kill. To kill the Germans. God is on our side . . . it is His will that the Germans be killed.

And in Germany, the good pastors called upon the Germans to kill the allies . . . to please the same God. That was a part of the general propaganda, built up to make people war conscious and murder conscious.

Beautiful ideals were painted for our boys who were sent out to die. This was the "war to end all wars." This was the "war to make the world safe for democracy." No one mentioned to them, as they marched away, that their going and their dying would mean huge war profits. No one told these American soldiers that they might be shot down by bullets made by their own brothers here. No one told them that the ships on which they were going to cross might be torpedoed by submarines built with United States patents. They were just told it was to be a "glorious adventure."

Thus, having stuffed patriotism down their throats, it was decided to make them help pay for the war, too. So, we gave them the large salary of $30 a month.

All they had to do for this munificent sum was to leave their dear ones behind, give up their jobs, lie in swampy trenches, eat canned willy (when they could get it) and kill and kill and kill . . . and be killed.

But wait!

Half of that wage (just a little more than a riveter in a shipyard or a laborer in a munitions factory safe at home made in a day) was promptly taken from him to support his dependents, so that they would not become a charge upon his community. Then we made him pay what amounted to accident insurance —

something the employer pays for in an enlightened state -and that cost him $6 a month. He had less than $9 a month left.

Then, the most crowning insolence of all — he was virtually blackjacked into paying for his own ammunition, clothing, and food by being made to buy Liberty Bonds. Most soldiers got no money at all on pay days.

We made them buy Liberty Bonds at $100 and then we bought them back — when they came back from the war and couldn't find work — at $84 and $86. And the soldiers bought about $2,000,000,000 worth of these bonds!

Yes, the soldier pays the greater part of the bill. His family pays too. They pay it in the same heart-break that he does. As he suffers, they suffer. At nights, as he lay in the trenches and watched shrapnel burst about him, they lay home in their beds and tossed sleeplessly — his father, his mother, his wife, his sisters, his brothers, his sons, and his daughters.

When he returned home minus an eye, or minus a leg or with his mind broken, they suffered too — as much as and even sometimes more than he. Yes, and they, too, contributed their dollars to the profits of the munitions makers and bankers and shipbuilders and the manufacturers and the speculators made. They, too, bought Liberty Bonds and contributed to the profit of the bankers after the Armistice in the hocus-pocus of manipulated Liberty Bond prices.

And even now the families of the wounded men and of the mentally broken and those who never were able to readjust themselves are still suffering and still paying.

CHAPTER FOUR

How To Smash

This Racket!

WELL, it's a racket, all right.

A few profit — and the many pay. But there is a way to stop it. You can't end it by disarmament conferences. You can't eliminate it by peace parleys at Geneva. Well-meaning but impractical groups can't wipe it out by resolutions. It can be smashed effectively only by taking the profit out of war.

The only way to smash this racket is to conscript capital and industry and labor before the nations manhood can be conscripted. One month before the Government can conscript the young men of the nation — it must conscript capital and industry and labor. Let the officers and the directors and the high-powered executives of our armament factories and our munitions makers and our shipbuilders and our airplane builders and the manufacturers of all the other things that provide profit in war time as well as the bankers and the speculators, be conscripted — to get $30 a month, the same wage as the lads in the trenches get.

Let the workers in these plants get the same wages — all the workers, all presidents, all executives, all directors, all managers, all bankers — yes, and all generals and all admirals and all officers and all politicians and all government office holders — everyone in the nation be restricted to a total monthly income not to exceed that paid to the soldier in the trenches!

Let all these kings and tycoons and masters of business and all those workers in industry and all our senators and governors and majors pay half of their monthly $30 wage to their families and pay war risk insurance and buy Liberty Bonds.

Why shouldn't they?

They aren't running any risk of being killed or of having their bodies mangled or their minds shattered. They aren't sleeping in muddy trenches. They aren't hungry. The soldiers are!

Give capital and industry and labor thirty days to think it over and you will find, by that time, there will be no war. That will smash the war racket — that and nothing else.

Maybe I am a little too optimistic. Capital still has some say. So capital won't permit the taking of the profit out of war until the people — those who do the suffering and still pay the price — make up their minds that those they elect to office shall do their bidding, and not that of the profiteers.

Another step necessary in this fight to smash the war racket is the limited plebiscite to determine whether a war should be declared. A plebiscite not of all the voters but merely of those who would be called upon to do the fighting and dying. There wouldn't be very much sense in having a 76-year-old president of a munitions factory or the flat-footed head of an international banking firm or the cross-eyed manager of a uniform manufacturing plant — all of whom see visions of tremendous profits in the event of war — voting on whether the nation should go to war or not. They never would be called upon to shoulder arms — to sleep in a trench and to be shot. Only those who would be called upon to risk their lives for their country should have the privilege of voting to determine whether the nation should go to war.

There is ample precedent for restricting the voting to those affected. Many of our states have restrictions on those permitted to vote. In most, it is necessary to be able to read and write before you may vote. In some, you must own property. It would be a simple matter each year for the men coming of military age to register in their communities as they did in the draft during the World War and be examined physically. Those who could pass and who would therefore be called upon to bear arms in the event of war would be eligible to vote in a limited plebiscite. They should be the ones to have the power to decide — and not a Congress few of whose members are within the age limit and fewer still of whom are in physical condition to bear arms. Only those who must suffer should have the right to vote.

A third step in this business of smashing the war racket is to make certain that our military forces are truly forces for defense only.

At each session of Congress the question of further naval appropriations comes up. The swivel-chair admirals of Washington (and there are always a lot of them) are very adroit lobbyists. And they are smart. They don't shout that "We need a lot of battleships to war on this nation or that nation." Oh no. First of all, they let it be known that America is menaced by a great naval power. Almost any day, these admirals will tell you, the great fleet of this supposed enemy will strike suddenly and annihilate 125,000,000 people. Just like that. Then they begin to cry for a larger navy. For what? To fight the enemy? Oh my, no. Oh, no. For defense purposes only.

Then, incidentally, they announce maneuvers in the Pacific. For defense. Uh, huh.

The Pacific is a great big ocean. We have a tremendous coastline on the Pacific. Will the maneuvers be off the coast, two or three hundred miles? Oh, no. The maneuvers will be two thousand, yes, perhaps even thirty-five hundred miles, off the coast.

The Japanese, a proud people, of course will be pleased beyond expression to see the united States fleet so close to Nippon's shores. Even as pleased as would be the residents of California were they to dimly discern through the morning mist, the Japanese fleet playing at war games off Los Angeles.

The ships of our navy, it can be seen, should be specifically limited, by law, to within 200 miles of our coastline. Had that been the law in 1898 the Maine would never have gone to Havana Harbor. She never would have been blown up. There would have been no war with Spain with its attendant loss of life. Two hundred miles is ample, in the opinion of experts, for defense purposes. Our nation cannot start an offensive war if its ships can't go further than 200 miles from the coastline. Planes might be permitted to go as far as 500 miles from the coast for purposes of reconnaissance. And the army should never leave the territorial limits of our nation.

To summarize: Three steps must be taken to smash the war racket.

1. We must take the profit out of war.

2. We must permit the youth of the land who would bear arms to decide whether or not there should be war.

3. We must limit our military forces to home defense purposes.

CHAPTER FIVE

To Hell With War!

I am not a fool as to believe that war is a thing of the past. I know the people do not want war, but there is no use in saying we cannot be pushed into another war.

Looking back, Woodrow Wilson was re-elected president in 1916 on a platform that he had "kept us out of war" and on the implied promise that he would "keep us out of war." Yet, five months later he asked Congress to declare war on Germany.

In that five-month interval the people had not been asked whether they had changed their minds. The 4,000,000 young men who put on uniforms and marched or sailed away were not asked whether they wanted to go forth to suffer and die.

Then what caused our government to change its mind so suddenly?

Money.

An allied commission, it may be recalled, came over shortly before the war declaration and called on the President. The President summoned a group of advisers. The head of the commission spoke. Stripped of its diplomatic language, this is what he told the President and his group:

"There is no use kidding ourselves any longer. The cause of the allies is lost. We now owe you (American bankers, American munitions makers, American manufacturers, American speculators, American exporters) five or six billion dollars.

If we lose (and without the help of the United States we must lose) we, England, France and Italy, cannot pay back this money . . . and Germany won't.

So . . . "

Had secrecy been outlawed as far as war negotiations were concerned, and had the press been invited to be present at that conference, or had radio been available to broadcast the proceedings, America never would have entered the World War. But this conference, like all war discussions, was shrouded in utmost secrecy. When our boys were sent off to war they were told it was a "war to make the world safe for democracy" and a "war to end all wars."

Well, eighteen years after, the world has less of democracy than it had then. Besides, what business is it of ours whether Russia or Germany or England or France or Italy or Austria live under democracies or monarchies? Whether they are Fascists or Communists? Our problem is to preserve our own democracy.

And very little, if anything, has been accomplished to assure us that the World War was really the war to end all wars.

Yes, we have had disarmament conferences and limitations of arms conferences. They don't mean a thing. One has just failed; the results of another have been nullified. We send our professional soldiers and our sailors and our politicians and our diplomats to these conferences. And what happens?

The professional soldiers and sailors don't want to disarm. No admiral wants to be without a ship. No general wants to be without a command. Both mean men without jobs. They are not for disarmament. They cannot be for limitations of arms. And at all these conferences, lurking in the background but all-powerful, just the same, are the sinister agents of those who profit by war. They see to it that these conferences do not disarm or seriously limit armaments.

The chief aim of any power at any of these conferences has not been to achieve disarmament to prevent war but rather to get more armament for itself and less for any potential foe.

There is only one way to disarm with any semblance of practicability. That is for all nations to get together and scrap every ship, every gun, every rifle, every tank, every war plane. Even this, if it were possible, would not be enough.

The next war, according to experts, will be fought not with battleships, not by artillery, not with rifles and not with machine guns. It will be fought with deadly chemicals and gases.

Secretly each nation is studying and perfecting newer and ghastlier means of annihilating its foes wholesale. Yes, ships will continue to be built, for the shipbuilders must make their profits. And guns still will be manufactured and powder and rifles will be made, for the munitions makers must make their huge profits. And the soldiers, of course, must wear uniforms, for the manufacturer must make their war profits too.

But victory or defeat will be determined by the skill and ingenuity of our scientists.

If we put them to work making poison gas and more and more fiendish mechanical and explosive instruments of destruction, they will have no time for the constructive job of building greater prosperity for all peoples. By putting them to this useful job, we can all make more money out of peace than we can out of war — even the munitions makers.

So...I say,

TO HELL WITH WAR!

Also available

Audiobook of *War Is A Racket* is exclusively available on Audible.com